HOW TO START YOUR OWN
MAKEUP OR BEAUTY BRAND
20 EASY STEPS TO FOLLOW
BY TWAMA NAMBILI

TABLE OF CONTENTS

GETTING STARTED

Hi there!

So you are looking to start a beauty brand and you don't know where to start? To be fair, many people in the beauty industry don't want to share most of these details with you. However, sharing knowledge is how we all grow. There is a lot that goes into creating a beauty brand—behind the scene things, that most people don't know to expect when wanting to start a makeup or beauty brand. Based on my experience, creating Pheora Rucci (which officially launches Fall 2019), I have written 20 top tips I know would help you in starting a solid foundation for you makeup or beauty brand. I learned these tips in a period of 2 years that I have spent building my brand; I dove in head first because I found it very hard to get assistance from people who have started beauty brands. None was willing to share their experiences with me, so I had to learn by trying, failing, and improving.

This book is technically only 6 pages long in a Microsoft word document, and it's only a **15 to 30 minute read**. I have made this book very visual, colourful, short, affordable and very easy to read or follow.

Remember,
You don't need everything to be perfect in order to start…you just need to start…start where you are!

Best Regards,
Twama Nambili

1. DO YOUR RESEARCH

As your start on your journey to creating a makeup or beauty brand, you want to make sure that you know the industry you want to enter inside-out. You want to know your competitors, their customers, their products, and their operations. You need to identify a need in the market and how you can best fill it. You want to know about the costs associated with manufacturing the product that you are thinking of. You want to find out about marketing, suppliers, and everything that can help you make better decisions. You want to research brand names, location, consumer behavior and so forth. Google is your friend in all of this, but it can also help to ask people who have experience in the same industry, if they are willing to share their knowledge.

2. IDENTIFY YOUR BUSINESS MODEL

A business model is very important because businesses need money to survive. How will your company make money? How will your brand trade? Will it be retail, e-commerce, or both? What would the supply chain look like? In essence, a business model is a company's plan for how it will generate revenues and make a profit. It explains what products or services the business plans to manufacture and market, and how it plans to do so, including what expenses it will incur.

3. DECIDE ON THE NAME AND LOGO

The name and logo are the brand's identity, and it is what customers see first. You want to think really hard about the name you want to create. Refrain from creating a brand name that is too long or too obnoxious. You want a name that is easy to remember, pronounce, and reflects what you want your brand to embody. It's okay to name the brand after yourself, too.

Get your logo professionally done, in a way that positively reflect on your brand. If you don't have a large budget, approach a graphic design student and offer them $30 to $50 to create a great logo for you. They can gain experience and some cash in the process. You can find graphic designers on www.linkedin.com or www.fiverr.com (you can get work done for as little at $5). If not, look at your network of friends and family, you might have one who will do it for free.

4. PICK A LOCATION

Based on your research, you should be able to identify what city and country you would like to launch your brand. Whatever location you select, it should work to the advantage of your business. You must think of the associated costs: salaries, office rent, taxes, registration, etc. If you have the funding, you can secure an office space, alternatively you can also use your home as a base of operations until you are in a position to afford an office space.

5. REGISTER YOUR COMPANY

There is usually no rush to register a company in your early stages, however, if you plan on securing funding or talking to suppliers—it can be helpful to have your company registered. Some manufacturers and investors would want to have your company registered before they can proceed negotiating with you. It also gives you legitimacy. Registering a business in the UK costs only £12 and in the US—costs can range between $50 to $1000, depending on the type of company and State you are registering it in.

6. CREATE A BUSINESS PLAN OR PITCH DECK

This is optional. You don't need a written business plan to start a business. That said, even if you choose not to write your plan down, you should have one in your mind. Because without a clear and concise plan or direction, your business will fail. Keep in mind that you will need a business plan if you want to secure funds from banks, venture capital firms, seed funds or private equity firms. In this case, keep the business plan short and sweet (10-12 pages is enough). Get to the point. It may be better to create a Pitch Deck, which you can easily send to investors.

Here are tips on how to write a great business plan:
https://www.allbusiness.com/what-does-a-business-plan-include-1740-1.html

Get free sample business plans here:
https://www.bplans.com/sample_business_plans.php

Learn how to create a pitch deck:
https://pitchdeck.improvepresentation.com/what-is-a-pitch-deck

7. FIND A MANUFACTURER

Once you have done your research on the industry and know what products you want manufactured, it's time to research and approach manufacturers. Try to shortlist your manufacturers from top 10, top 5, and then top 2. Talk to the manufacturers and ask for samples. You should avoid manufacturers that will charge you for samples, except for shipping. The best recommendation is to meet these manufacturers face-to-face and tour their factories. If you do not have the funds for that, samples are also a great way to go.

Countries that are reputable in cosmetic manufacturing are Italy, France, Germany, US, China, Korea, and Malaysia. So, you would want to search for manufacturers there. Google is your friend. Really, it is! For China, alibaba.com is helpful, however; be very careful. This is an option, but I would recommend that if you choose a Chinese factory, you should plan to visit their factory to see their manufacturing standards and the ingredients they use. This is a quality check that will save you money in the long-run and also prevent you from getting scammed.

Keep in mind that most manufacturers will have a **Minimum Quantity Order** (MQO) per SKU, this can range from 100 to 10,000 (depending on the size of the manufacturer) units per SKU. A **Stock Keeping Unit** (SKU) is a product and service identification code for a store or product, often displayed as a machine-readable bar code that helps track the item for inventory. Let me simplify that: if you want to sell 1 lipstick formula, that comes in 5 different colors, then you have 5 SKUs. If the MQO per SKU, from your manufacturer, is 100 per SKU—then this means that you would need to order a minimum of 500 units from this supplier, if you want all 5 colors.

If you do not have a lot of money, I highly recommend that you start with something small. That's something I had to learn the hard way, because initially I wanted to have it all! Start with something like false eyelashes or 4 color lipsticks. Then start adding more products to your brand over time.

Once you decided your manufacturer, it's time to choose your formulas. You have to decide whether you will go with Private Label (using an existing formula) or creating your own formula from scratch (my preferred option). Many makeup brands you see on the shelves today are private label or have one or two products that are private label. Creating your own formula costs more and takes a long time (9-12 month), however, you will have a formula that none else has. Most brands starting up use private label and move into creating their own formulas. If you can afford it, opt for creating your own formula. You can reduce the costs by increasing your MQO.

9. BUDGET AND SECURE FUNDING

If you have done your research right, and if you have a business plan (in your mind or written), then you should have identified how much it would cost for you to start and run your business. It's important for you to budget realistically and keep to that budget.

If you don't already have your own funding, you would need to raise funds. There are many avenues from which to raise the funds—crowdfunding (Kickstarter, Indiegodo, Seedrs, Crowdcube, GoFundme, etc), bank loans, private equity, venture capital, seed funding, angel investment, or family&friends. It's very difficult to raise funds from banks, private equity or venture capital firms for a start-up beauty brand with no proven sales. Unless you have a patent or personally know partners at these firms, raising funds from friends or angel investors may be your best bet—at least until you have proven sales that would appeal to large investors. Take note that, unless you already have the right connections, it is very difficult to raise funds from investors for beauty products without having a determined formula or prototype. Try to work out your formulas first before approaching investors. Also try to launch with one product.

10. BRAINSTORM COLOR AND NAMES

You would want to figure out how your product should look like. What color would it be and what name(s) should it have? You want to think about what will appeal to your target customer. Pick appealing color and names, and have fun with it!

11. PACKAGING

Once you have a formula, you must work on your packaging. Packaging for each product would vary. For foundation, for example; you would need a bottle that would hold the formula and the paper packaging that the bottle will be in. In some cases, you may need to source the bottle and the paper packaging yourself. It's very important that at this stage you hire a packaging designer. If you can't afford to or don't have the time for this, most (not all) manufacturers will offer an inclusive service where they also source all of the packaging for you, at an extra fee. If you are using a Chinese manufacturer, this fee will tend to be very small and you may not even notice it at all. Regardless, you will still need to hire a copywriter to write the description of your products on all your packaging. The manufacturers do not do this for you. LinkedIn is your friend when it comes to hiring any employee you may want.

12. KNOW ABOUT FDA REGULATION (US) AND EU REGULATIONS

If you plan to sell your product(s) in the US or EU, you need to make sure that they comply with safety regulations. You need to make sure that you know the ingredients in your product(s) and that they comply. I would particularly caution when working with a Chinese manufacturer, or manufacturer outside of these areas, that you ask them whether their products meet the standards set by the EMA (EU) and FDA. Don't just take their words for it, you can get the products independently tested by an expert to see the ingredients. If you don't have the money, approach a chemistry and biology professor at a university or college near you. Don't take chances, you may lose money if your product(s) are seized by customs or you may get sued for harming someone with your product(s).

Also, don't make any claims until they can be scientifically backed up—that is false advertising and it is illegal!

13. DECIDE PRODUCT PRICING

In your business model, you should have decided on what your products are and how much they are going to cost. The product price should include your cost of goods sold (how much it cost you to manufacturer the product, including shipping and packaging), and of course your profit margin (what you will make). You should think carefully about your price points and compare that to your target customers to see if it makes sense. If your target audience is lower middle class, it doesn't make sense to make a foundation priced at $50, vice versa. $10 may be a more reasonable. If you are having a hard time calculating your prices, you can also look at what similar products currently costs (based on quality, etc) in the market, and this can guide you on how you can price your product(s).

14. E-COMMERCE WEBSITE

We are in a digital era, you would want to have an online presence. So, you want to give people an opportunity to order your products online. There are so many successful beauty brands that started online—Juvia's place, Jeffreestar Cosmetics, Huda Beauty, etc. This of course would depend on your target market. If your target customers don't use the internet, then maybe an e-commerce website is not practical.

Useful sites:
www.bluehost.com if you want to host your own website, they also sell domains.
www.themeforest.net for affordable themes for your website.
www.wix.com if you want something fast, easy, and hustle-free.
www.shopify.com if you are looking for an e-commerce platform to sell your products and easily manage your sales. You can do all of these with wix or Bluehost, but it's just a bit more convenient with Shopify. Shopify costs $29.99 per month.

15. CREATE A MARKETING STRATEGY

Besides funding, a marketing strategy should be the heart of your business. This strategy should tell you how you will get in front your target consumer. Who is your customer? What do they like? What is their income level? How do you get their attention?

You can start working on your marketing strategy once you have a business model down, and refine it as you go along the process of sourcing and manufacturing.

In your plan, you should also allocate a handsome budget to marketing, whether it be traditional media or digital marketing. Given that majority of the people are online, it would make sense allocate a significant sum to social media marketing. But this will also depend on where you live. If you live in places like Africa or Latin America, where radio and newspapers are still king, then allocate your budget towards that.

16. IDENTIFY A FULFILMENT CENTER OR WAREHOUSE

Depending on the magnitude at which you aim to launch your brand, you may need a warehouse (to store your inventory) and a fulfilment center (to send out your orders). You can find companies that offer both services. If you are starting small, you can do all of this from your home until you get to a point where you are no longer able to handle the orders yourself. If you decide to go with a third party, keep in mind that this comes at significant costs. A fulfilment center is great because they would generally have great shipping rates and will know how to clear customs in various countries. You need to anticipate your sales and you should aim to negotiate with these centers because it doesn't make sense to keep losing money in center costs when the business is not generating revenues.

17. IDENTIFY YOUR SHIPPING COSTS

You should identify how much each product will cost you to ship from a manufacturer (including customs) and to ship to a customer, because you also need to include this in your product pricing. To save money, you can generally negotiate a low rate with your local FedEx, USPS, UPS, Royal Mail, or DHL for sending bulk orders. If you go with a fulfilment center, the fulfilment center should have these deals already set in stone. If you think you can get better rates by talking directly to the shipping company, then do that.

18. BUILD AN AUDIENCE

Before you launch, you want to make sure that you already have people anticipating your product. This is the time to sit down and build your brand's story, then take it to the world. There are many ways to build an audience:

1) Create a landing page, which gives a short overview of your product/brand and put an option for people to subscribe to your newsletter. You can get a free landing page on www.wix.com – and for $75, you can get your own domain and professional site that has no ads.
2) You can create a free newsletter opt-in with www.mailchimp.com. Be sure to send regular updates.
3) Build a community. Create a social media following. Focus your efforts on Instagram, Facebook, and YouTube. Make sure that you create content that people love, and make sure that it's content your target customer would like.
4) Tell friends and family, and get them to share your social media handles and subscribe.
5) Offer people something of value in exchange for their emails. Giving useful content for free or doing giveaways is another great way to precure and build your newsletter.

You would want to have a team that understands your brand's vision and will ensure it succeeds. If you have money, you can hire these individuals, and if you are starting from home—get help from friends and family or hire employees in exchange for equity. You would at least need a lawyer, an accountant, a digital marketing manager or marketing manager, a PR firm, a copywriter, a sales manager, and a packaging designer. Some of these skills can be outsourced—legal work, copywriting, packaging design, and PR. However, you should keep in mind that outsourcing work can also cost a lot in the long run if you are using it too often, and it may be best to hire an employee instead. Take a look at your financial standing, the amount of work required and decide what is best for you and your business.

LinkedIn is a large database. To get exactly what you want, you can customize your query. If you want to find a Digital Marketing Manager who is interested in the beauty industry, currently works at MAC Cosmetics and located in New York City, I would enter the following in the search box: "Digital Marketing Manager" and "Beauty". Then for currently company, enter MAC Cosmetics and then under location, add New York City. This technique, which I learned from a friend, has saved me a lot of time and effort.

20. IT'S TIME TO LAUNCH!

Once you have your team, your product(s), and your marketing strategy in mind, it's time to launch. Make sure that you have a great launch and that the audience you spend time cultivating knows that you have launched. Put your marketing team to work! All the best!

FINAL WORDS...

I hope that you found this book and the information within it meaningful. Remember that the beauty industry is one of the easiest industries to enter because it does not require you to have a lot of money to get started. But that also means you will have a lot of competition, so you need to find ways to set yourself apart from your competitors, by building a solid foundation.

Remember, you don't need to have everything perfect to start....just start! If you wait for everything to be perfect, you will never start. So, start! You will figure out the rest during the journey.

If you have follow-up questions, you can contact me by visiting:

I wish you all the best with your business venture. I look forward to seeing your brand(s).

Best Regards
Twama Nambili

Everything is a state of mind.

Whether you think you can, or think that you cannot— you are right.

www.ingramcontent.com/pod-product-compliance
Lightning Source LLC
Chambersburg PA
CBHW041212180526
45172CB00006B/1248